UNDENIABLY DAWG

when barking at total strangers in public feels perfectly natural

A Haiku Hunker-Fest Written and Illustrated by

DAVE HELWIG

d

Hill Street Press
Athens, Georgia

A HILL STREET PRESS BOOK

Published in the United States of America by Hill Street Press LLC
191 East Broad Street, Suite 216 • Athens, Georgia 30601-2848 USA

706.713.7200 • info@hillstreetpress.com • www.hillstreetpress.com

Hill Street Press is committed to preserving the written word. Every effort is made to print books on acid-free paper with post-consumer recycled content.

Hill Street Press books are available in bulk purchase and customized editions to institutions and companies. Please contact us for more information.

Text and jacket design by Andy McIntire and Jenifer Carter.

Library of Congress Cataloging-In-Publication Data
Library of Congress Cataloging-in-Publication Data

Helwig, Dave, 1958-
 Undeniably dawg : when barking at total strangers in public feels
perfectly natural / by Dave Helwig.
    p. cm.
 ISBN 1-58818-126-X (alk. paper)
 1. University of Georgia.--Football--Miscellanea. 2. Georgia Bulldogs
(Football team)--Miscellanea. 3. University of Georgia.--Football--Poetry.
4. Georgia Bulldogs (Football team)--Poetry. I. Title.
 GV958.G42H45 2006
 796.332'630975818--dc22

                        2006026870

ISBN-10: 1-58818-126-X
ISBN-13: 978-1-58818-126-8

10 9 8 7 6 5 4 3 2 1

First printing

ACKNOWLEDGEMENTS

I must thank my family for their love and support. Every time I come up with another hair-brained idea (and that's amazingly difficult as bald as I am) the response is always "Go for it. You'll make it work".

To my close friend, Barry Every, for his . . . shall we say, interestingly weird, dry, and sarcastic sense of humor. It can only be explained as somewhere between less filling and tastes great. It's an aquired taste. Keep me rollin', Buddy.

I thank Andy McIntire, whom I have come to know as friend, gifted cartoonist, and part-time juggler. There's a long list of other really peculiar things I could list that he enjoys for entertainment, but none would believe me anyway. His dedication and input during the layout of this book went above and beyond the call of duty. I'm only saying these nice things about him because he has a cool dog.

I must thank my daughter, Tara. A great Dawg fan and the reason for anything good I've ever done in my life. HOW 'BOUT THEM DAWGS, Kiddo.

I suppose I should go ahead and thank my brother, Steve for picking the Gators as his team all those years ago. It pointed me on a clear path . . . as far away from those ORANGE AND BLUE CLAD . . . BELLY.

INTRODUCTION

I assume that the first question you ask is …Why haiku? The next question would logically be …What the heck is a haiku?

As I understand it from a reliable source (a drunken sushi chef I once met watching a Georgia football game at one of Athens' fine establishments), haiku is loosely defined as a form of poetry with five syllables in the first line, followed by seven in the second, and finishing with five again in the third and final line.

The reasons I chose haiku for this book are as follows:
1.   I'm not a novelist. I'm a cartoonist.
2.   The thing doesn't have to rhyme.
3.   Haiku, being comprised of short little thoughts, lend themselves nicely to my short attention span and lack of patience.

In my own defense on that third point…it's difficult to concentrate on anything but the Dawgs when football season is in full swing and even harder in the off-season when you're bored and wondering …Why the heck do we have to wait so long for it to start again? I don't think anyone would really complain if we just skipped from the end of the bowl games on through to Picture Day. It's usually too cold or too hot to put up with those months, anyway.

I've been barking for the Georgia Bulldogs as long as I can remember. I have a vague recollection of my older brother picking the Florida Gators as his team of choice. Out of a strong sense of sibling rivalry I latched onto the Dawgs. I should thank him for that some day. Today, we get along much better, except for the week of the annual border bash in Jacksonville, which we have dubbed HATE WEEK.

It's difficult to express how much I enjoy what I do. It's a blessing to creatively combine my obsessions. Besides my daughter, Tara (a huge Dawg fan, herself) there is nothing I am more passionate about than art and the Dawgs. I have had a wonderful time working on *UNDENIABLY DAWG*. The result is a strange cocktail that is both curious and refreshing, like a having a light beer in a martini glass with an olive and one of those little umbrellas.

Besides wanting to entertain the Georgia faithful, my main goal in creating this book is to irritate those who don't have enough sense to pull for the greatest team there is in all the land.*

With that thought in mind, I would like to dedicate this book to my brother, Steve (the Gator fan) because it will really piss him off.

GO DAWGS!

* The opinions expressed here are those of the author of this book and give or take ninety thousand of his closest friends on any glorious Georgia Football Saturday.

THE JOURNEY

Every goose-bump on your body is tingling with anticipation.

Load the truck for a Bulldog weekend.
Coolers, grill, chairs, boom box and the big red tent.
Think we have enough ice?

Getting there is half the fun.

You might even invite the neighbor who roots for Tech.
I wouldn't recommend it, but if you do...
Make him ride in the bed so he'll get bugs stuck in his teeth.
He'll feel more at home that way.

It's a Bulldog caravan.

A road trip's ahead
Could get there with my eyes closed
You drive. I'm sleeping.

Can't wait to get there
The Dawgs are calling me home
Just live in Bogart

Couldn't get to sleep
Too wound up about the trip
I need more coffee

I have the tickets
Cooler is stocked and loaded
Damn, forgot the wife.

Got my bulldog hat
My bulldog shirt, pants, and socks
You should see my thong

Flags flying proudly
Got the big "G's" on both sides
God, it's beautiful

Came down from up north
Cousin pulls for the Buckeyes
I just think he's nuts

Rode with a "VOL" fan
Can't bear "Rocky Top" again
He'll take the bus home

Atlanta Highway
Hang a right on Lumpkin Street
Promised land...turn left

What a traffic jam
Larry's on the radio
Turn it up, will you?

Dawg fans headed home
The parting of the red sea
We'll be back next week

THE GATHERING

You can smell the burgers as they dance and glisten on the grill.

Everyone is talking about how the defense
has to hold the line to pull this one off.

Munson is getting us all worked up on the pre-game show.

Toss me that ball, son and go deep.

Cold drinks and hot topics.

We've been tailgating here since Herschel was in diapers.

Good friends and good times
A family reunion
Bulldog family

Trolling for a space
Stop the car! That one's perfect
Package store next door

Let's crank up the grill
Dude, I can't see anything
Hold that flashlight still

Smell of Bar-B-Q
There's cold beer in the cooler
Forgot the cooler

Love our tailgate spot
This is nicer than our yard
Let's just move in here

Come and grab a plate
You say you're a Gamecock fan
That'll be ten bucks

Don't have a ticket
It's just me and Munson now
Tailgate nirvana

Stomachs are all full
March of the Bulldog Nation
Ain't missin' kickoff

That was a great game
The Bulldogs are on a roll
Pass me a roll, please

The car's all packed up
Handshakes and hugs all around
See ya'll here next week

THE EXPERIENCE

Athens, Georgia on a sun drenched autumn Saturday
is the closest thing to a country carnival
on the doorsteps of heaven.

The only things missing are the pigs and the freak show.

Wait a minute.

If Arkansas is in town and the frat boys
have been hitting the "liquid inspiration"
a bit too enthusiastically…

Ok, there is no difference.

Pretty girls in red
Blows a kiss to one or two
Grandma whacks Grandpa

Somebody slap me
I'm in Athens on game day
Not so hard next time

Athens in the fall
There is barking in the air
Great to be a Dawg

Look at all that red.
Go Dawgs, sic 'em woof woof woof!
I feel better, now

St. Louis has one
Mc Donalds' are all golden
I like ours better

Mighty pretty sight
Black "G" on a field of red
Orange makes me squint

All in red and black
Stripes plaids solids you name it
A fashion statement

Downtown Friday night
See old friends and make new ones
This round is on me

Redcoats are comin'
Glory glory to Georgia
The song of the south

Bulldog Nation cheers
Coach Right is leading 'em in
Can't beat the "Dawgwalk"

The homecoming game
Time to relive the old days
A fountain of youth

This one tops them all
Best college town in the land
Gainesville is a dump

It's the Red Clay Hounds
Comin' at you with teeth barred
Feel that Bulldog bite

Sanford Stadium
Ninety-thousand barking fans
And I'm one of them

Red and Black canines
THE dogs of college football
Others are just mutts

THE ENEMY

Look at that bunch of goobers
in their orange-checkered overalls.

I can't believe their momma let's them
dress like that in public.

Hey Boudreux! Lose the beads.
Mardi Gras ain't 'til February.

I'm glad my mascot ain't a chicken.
Can I have a drumstick?

Nice pocket protector, bug boy.

If I hear "Roll Tide" one more time, I swear…

Go back to the swamp where you belong, lizard lips!

I'm not a Gator !
I'll never be a Gator !
Clear enough for ya'?

Something sure does stink
Smells like a rancid dumpster
Must be a Gator

Bulldogs and Tigers
The South's oldest rivalry
A long time to hate

The Auburn Tigers
Alabama cow college
Hey, Bubba. Got milk?

Tigers? War Eagles?
Auburn University
Just choose ONE, will ya'!

North Avenue Bug
Lowlife invertebrate
Worse than a cockroach

Kind of pathetic
Can't fill your own stadium
Take out some more seats

The old Ramblin' Wreck
High maintenance and ugly
Like your cheerleaders

Hey, do the math, bug
Star Trek slide rule velcro shoes
Ain't gettin' a date

Dawgs stomp the insects
Great way to end the season
It's called pest control

If a Gamecock throws...
and the pass goes out of bounds...
is that a "fowl" ball?

Ya'll want some chicken?
Carolina is in town
Bite that chicken twice

Look at Clem and son
Conjures up visions, don't it?
A real knee slapper

Bacon, ham, sausage
Perhaps a nice grilled pork roast
Arkansas got smoked

Those Nashville Vandys
S.E.C. bottom dwellers
Gracious in defeat

Bayou Bengal cats
Gumbo snortin' so and so's
Geaux suck a crawfish

Bluegrass kitty cats
They sure play good basketball
Do they play football?

Starkeville kennel hound
What a mangy lookin' mutt
There's only ONE Dawg

Dawgs go to Oxford
Ole Miss in a heap of hurt
Hear that Rebel yell

Good Ole Rocky Snot
Sportin' your prison orange
Go clean the highway

Knoxville rifleman
The king of the wild frontier
Volunteer to bathe

Crockett's coonskin cap
Think it's a mullet toupee?
Roadkill on your head

Volunteer Navy
Floatin' on a garbage barge
Tennessee River rats

I beg your pardon
We're sorry, Lynyrd Skynyrd
Bama ain't so sweet

Big red elephants
Tuscaloosa Pachyderms
A herd of Dumbos

The Crimson Tide
Little Billy saves the day
We are MAN ENOUGH

THE DOG

Is that him? Look over there!

Lift me up on your shoulders so I can see him better, Daddy.

I just wanna give him a big ole' hug.

He looks really handsome in that red sweater.

Can we get one just like him?
I know…there's only one Uga.

Do you think they'll let me pet him?

I think he just winked at me. Did you see that?

I love that dog.

Got a shoved in face
Short, stocky, wrinkled and pale
A beautiful dog

Wears a red sweater
Adored by countless thousands
King of the junkyard

Air-conditioned house
Big bags of ice to lounge on
That's one cool canine

He's a movie star
A magazine cover boy
I wanna be him

Westminster dog show
Uga should enter next year
It wouldn't be close

Just look at that face
He's grinnin' from ear to ear
He knows that we won

A five hour drive
All the way from Savannah
Wouldn't miss a game

We think he's handsome
My brother thinks he's ugly
Go kiss a gator!

Can't believe my eyes
Almost bit that Auburn guy
Try again, Uga!

That's a Damn Good Dawg
Best mascot in all the land
Thanks a lot, Sonny

THE VOICE

There ain't nothin' or no one anywhere else like him.

Even if you've never been to a game,
he'd make you feel like you're on the fifty-yard line.

That voice sounds like gravel
rolling down a river of molasses.

Neutral? He doesn't know the meaning of the word.
I wouldn't have it any other way.

Turn up the radio a bit.
I don't want to miss a thing he says.

You never know when the next call will be a classic.

The game's on T.V.
Please turn off the talking heads
Rather hear Munson

A distinctive voice
It's gruff with lots of passion
Music to my ears

Question often asked
Hey, Loran…what do ya' got?
Never said pizza

Look at Old Smokey
Face will never be the same
Was hobnail booted

This is our last chance
Green lets it fly to Veron
Oh God! A touchdown!

Now, hunker down, Dawgs
You know what has to be done
Didn't mean to beg

Falling from the sky
That wasn't in the forecast
It's Dixie Crystals

Loves to go fishin'
Talks about it all the time
Should drop him a line

Buck to Lindsey...Scores!
Went right through that metal chair
Gator Bowl is junk, now

He's such a homer
The voice of the Dawg faithful
We love you, Larry

THE LEGENDS

DAVE HELWIG

My Grampa said he was at that game.
Leather helmets…really?
They called that play the "Flea Flicker".

Good Lord, that was at least twenty-five years ago.
Seems like only yesterday.

He was the greatest I ever saw wearing the Silver Britches.
I think I still have a program from that game.

They don't make them like that any more.
I was on the railroad track that day. What a game.

Hey, they named the building after him.
Those were great times.

Sinkwich and Trippi
Like trying to catch the wind
A strong southern wind

That's Coach Vince Dooley
Didn't he go to Auburn?
Who cares? He's ours, now.

Why does he do that?
His head is all bloodied up
Russells' junkyard Dawgs

Look at Dooleys' Dawgs
Irish eyes ain't smilin' now
Glory days are here

Cool as ice out there
A legend in the making
He's got the "Richt Stuff"

He's an Athens' boy
I saw him play at the "Y"
Lil' Fran Tarkentan

Get out of the way!
Herschel Walker has the ball
Bill Bates will tell you

Don't throw it his way
He has a nose for the ball
Kind of a ball Hogue

Nation's best player
Heisman voters got it right
Wrightsville should be proud

Who would have thunk it?
Just a couple of Davids
Broke all those records

Any Saturday
That's Georgia Bulldog football
Legends are born here

THE J'VILLE INVASION

We're going down on Monday. Gonna make a week of it.

Tie that rubber gator good and tight to the bumper, now.
You don't want it to fall off.

What time is your cousin meeting us in St. Simons?

We're gonna kick the chomp right out of 'em this year!

See you at Hooters at the Landing at seven.
It's your turn to buy the first round.

R.V. City will be rockin' tonight!
My tailgate spot is right next to the river.

Wear your red to the game tomorrow.
Everyone knows how well it clashes with orange.

No! You can't spell it with a "ph" either.

IT'S GREAT…TO BE…A GATOR HATER!

Palm trees and pig skins
Red and black, orange and blue
Pour me a cocktail

Pack up the R.V.
We're headed south for a fight
Watch out, Florida

This is amazing
Half is them and half is us
A whole lot of hate

Tied it on a string
Dragged it through the mud all day
Stomp on that gator

Got great seats today
Smack in the Gator section
Gonna be a fight

It's like a circus
Complete with clowns in orange
Not as funny, though

Jacksonville Bulldogs
Deep behind enemy lines
A victory dive

Need a miracle
Buck Belue to Lindsey Scott
I need some clean shorts

Woke up in my truck
I can't find my shoes or pants
Dawgs whooped the Gators

The St. Johns at night
Lights dancing on the river
Dancing for the Dawgs

A great tradition
Legendary rivalry
And what a party!

THE JUBILATION

I can hardly contain myself.
What an amazing come back!
I thought we were dead and buried.

High fives and kisses and hugs and…
what was your name again?

Can you believe what we just witnessed?
That might be the best game I've ever seen.
I'm getting all choked up here.

It's great …to be… a Georgia Bulldog!

Pay up, Bub!

There's going to be some property destroyed tonight!

Wow, what a finish
I knew they had it in 'em
Dawg day afternoon

What's that noise outside?
Oh, that's only my husband
Dawgs beat the Jackets

Dawgs just won ten straight
An amazing winning streak
Who else wants to streak?

Gonna go downtown
Gotta be with Dawg people
Gonna bark 'til dawn

On a winning streak
Wearing red Fruit of the Looms
Getting a bit ripe

There's no holding back
I feel a dance coming on
Bulldog conga line

A toast to the Dawgs
We could do no wrong today
Ring that chapel bell

Time to celebrate
I'm so happy I could burst
Which way's the restroom?

Hey there, Gator fan
You want to hear it again?
Just run Lindsey, run

The sun shines brighter
The sky seems much bluer, too
Tech loses again!

At the Georgia Dome
Waited twenty years for this
Gonna soak it up

Say it one more time
Dawgs...S.E.C. champions
Shut up and kiss me

If I had to choose
I'd pick winning every time
Losing really sucks!

THE AGONY

I swear, driving back after a game like that
takes twice as long as it did to get there.

I don't know what happened out there today.
Our guys fought hard though.

I can't stand losing to THEM!
I'm going to hear about it at work all year long.

What's the going rate to buy a referee these days?
Some of those calls couldn't be
anything but home cookin'.

They were holding Pollack all day long.

Don't talk to me right now. I need a moment alone.
If one of those orange clad jokers
so much as looks at me crosseyed…

Just get in the car. It's just a game?!
Get your own ride home.

Pass in the end zone
What do you mean…out of bounds?
Where are my Rolaids?

He lines up the kick
Tension is unbearable
Time for a quick prayer

The clouds are heavy
Darkness is consuming me
The Dawgs came up short

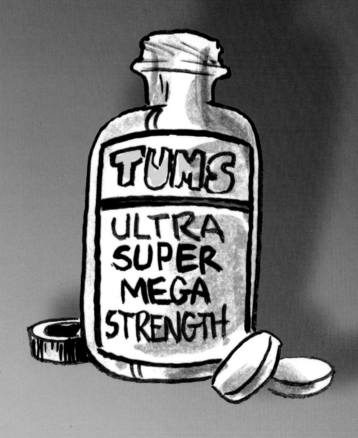

Fourth and goal to go
Everything rides on this play
I can't bear to watch

This is really sad
Never heard it so quiet
It's the Sanford blues

Why do I do this?
It hurts so bad when we lose
Uh…masochism?

I can't stand palm trees
No more orange juice for me
I loathe Florida

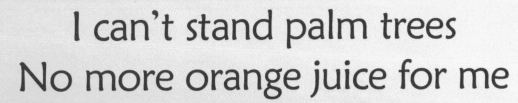

Anyone hungry?
Can't eat at a time like this
Just hand me a beer

This is degrading
Have to wear orange all week
What a stupid bet

My heart can't take it
I ain't never comin' back!
Auburn next week...hmm

WOOF!

THE RELATIONS

I love my wife…I love my family.
Just keep repeating that to yourself.

Sometime you can't tell about folks
at first glance…
or after you marry 'em.

Tell me your sister didn't just say "War Eagle".

Can't you get him to quit wearing
that putrid orange thing?
Stupid is as stupid does…STUPID!

Momma always used to say,
"You can't read a book buy it's cover".
Your husband can't read at all.
He went to 'Bama.

She roots for who?
Call my lawyer and bring me my shotgun!

My daughters' first game
Daddys' little girl just barked
And a glad tear falls

A newborn baby
Hope she never pulls for Tech
Spank her twice for luck

Grampa is a Dawg
Momma and Daddy are, too
Brother's a lizard

Can't keep my focus
I'd rather be at the game
"You may kiss the bride".

My husband's a dope
He loves the Yellow Jackets
I'd love a divorce

This takes some practice
I have to keep a straight face
Wife went to Vandy

Met her at a game
She was barking for the Dawgs
Love at first woof

She loves the Bulldogs
Punched a VOL fan in the face
Will you marry me?

He cries when we lose
And barks every time we win
Strong AND sensitive

My girlfriend dumped me
And I got my dang car towed
Who cares? The Dawgs won!

Choose the Dawgs or me!
Go to that game and we're through!
I miss her cornbread

What was that you said?
You don't want to hear me bark?
Get off of my porch

Man, what a body!
She's smart, rich…but a Gator
Back to the swamp, skank

Used to be married
Discovered he loves Bama
Pachyderm Pre-nup

A house divided
I'm a Dawg…he's a Gator
My momma warned me

THE DAWG BITES

Just random thoughts, really.
I'm always thinking about the Dawgs
One way or another.

They should put that on a bumper sticker.
I wish I would've come up with that one.
Wait…I think I did.

Did you hear the one about the Gator fan
and the herd of rabid hamsters?
I forget how that one goes, exactly.

What in the heck
were we talking about, anyway?

Oh, yeah…GO DAWGS!

Got a Chihuahua
He's small but tough and mean
He thinks he's Uga

If I was a dog…
Wait. I bark on Saturdays
Damn! I am a Dawg

We're 'tween the hedges
It's almost like a church here
God must love the Dawgs

There's a game this week
But, I called in sick last week
I'm calling in dead

Big man on campus
Cheerleaders all over me
Wake up! The game's on.

I root for the Dawgs
I've followed them all my life
Tech fans are clueless

Wish I had more space
My Bulldog room overflows
I'm adding a wing